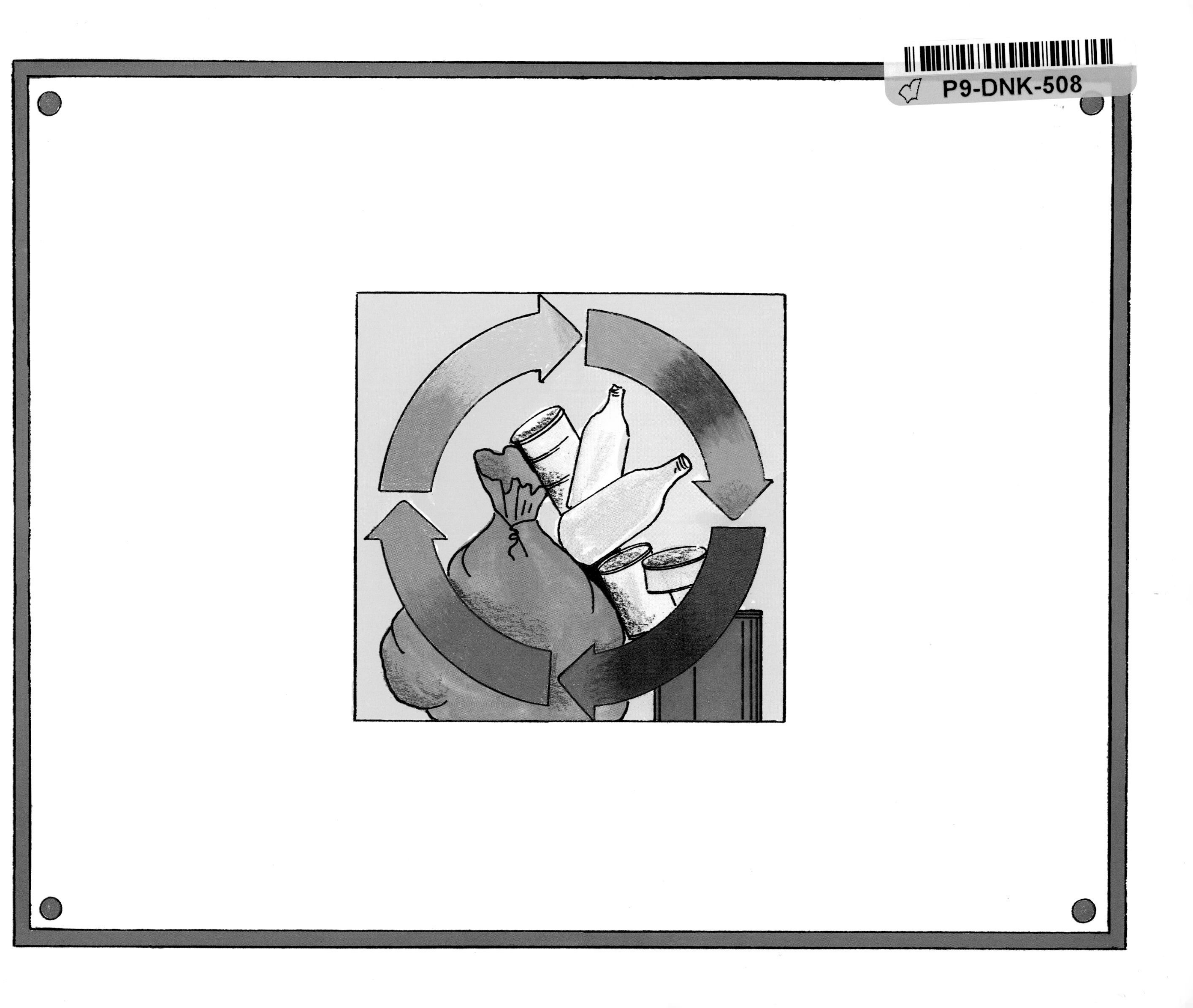

RECYCLE!
A HANDBOOK FOR KIDS

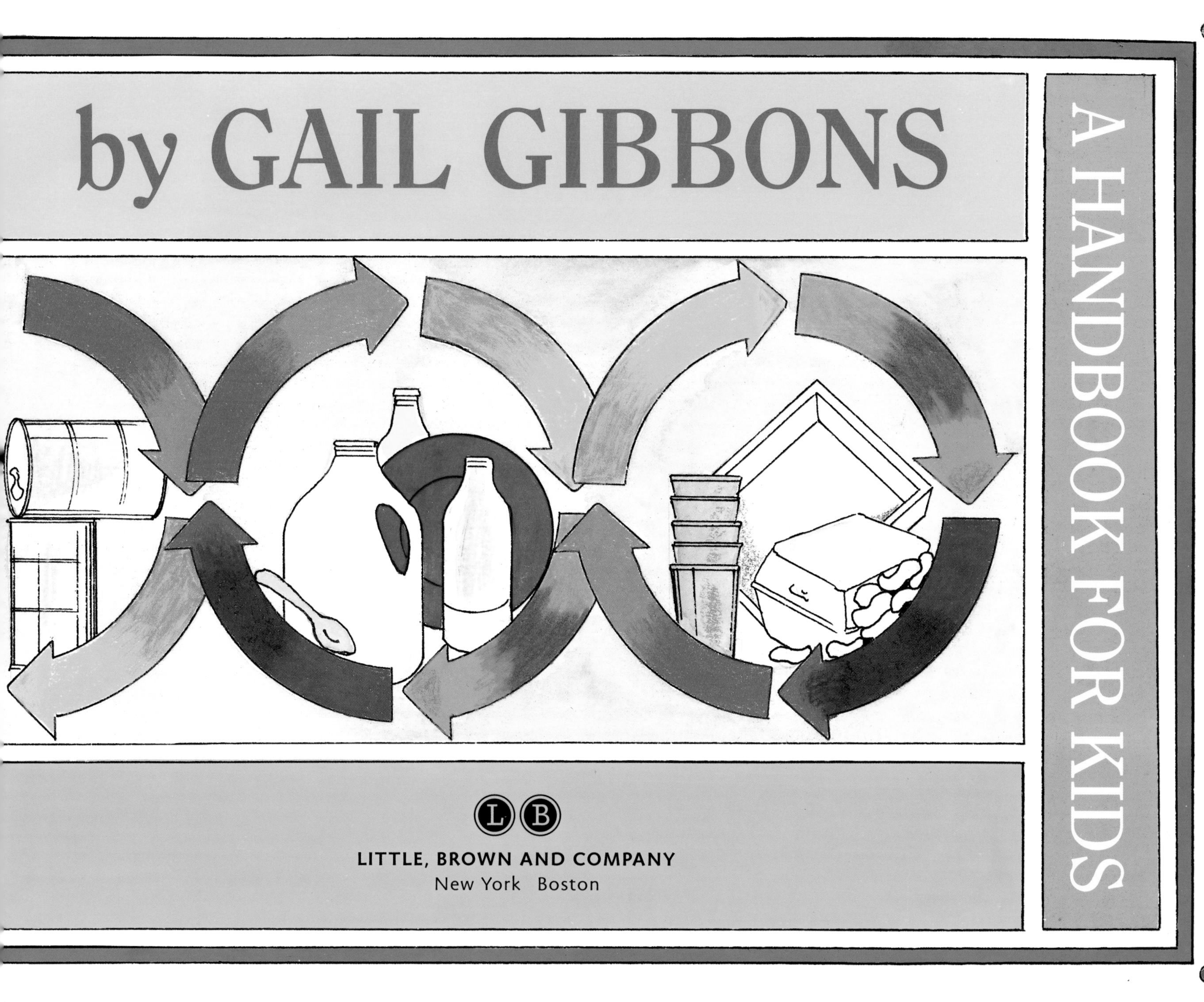
by GAIL GIBBONS
A HANDBOOK FOR KIDS
LB
LITTLE, BROWN AND COMPANY
New York Boston

To recyclers everywhere

Special thanks to Lisa Young,
the recycling public outreach coordinator
of the state of Vermont

Little, Brown and Company

Hachette Book Group
237 Park Avenue, New York, NY 10017
Visit our website at www.lb-kids.com

Little, Brown and Company is a division of Hachette Book Group, Inc.
The Little, Brown name and logo are trademarks of Hachette Book Group, Inc.

First Paperback Edition: April 1996
First published in hardcover in April 1992 by Little, Brown and Company

Library of Congress Cataloging-in-Publication Data

Gibbons, Gail.
Recycle! : a handbook for kids / by Gail Gibbons.—1st ed.
p. cm.
Summary: Explains the process of recycling from start to finish and discusses what happens to paper, glass, aluminum cans, and plastic when they are recycled into new products.
ISBN 978-0-316-30943-1
1. Recycling (Waste, etc.) — Juvenile literature. [1. Recycling (Waste)] I. Title.
TD794.5.G5 1992 91-4317
628.4'458 — dc20

20 19 18 17

SC

Manufactured in China

More and more garbage! Every day people throw more trash away. As the world population increases, *more* people throw more trash away. Garbage trucks come to pick it up, but where does all this trash go?

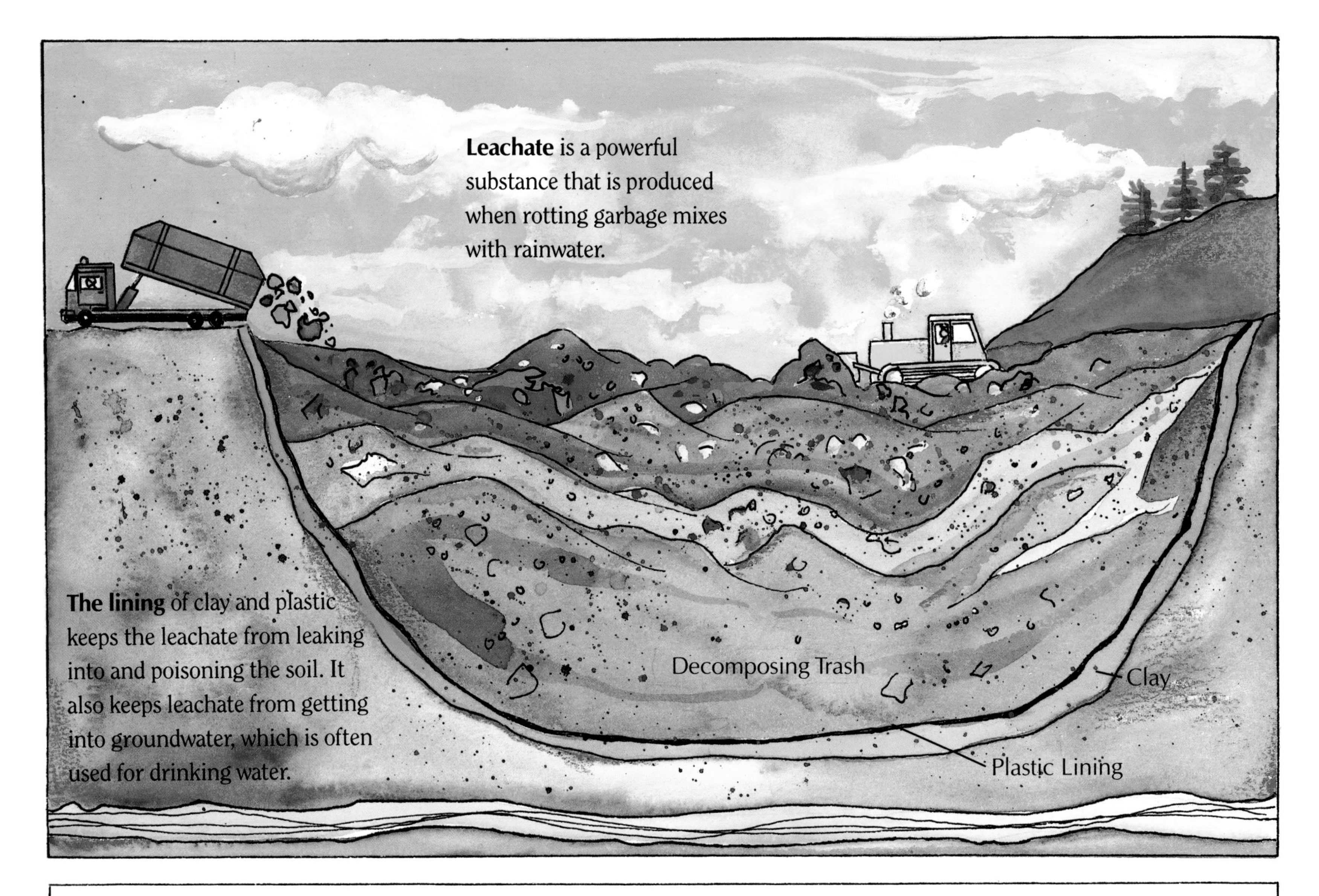

Most of it is hauled away to sanitary landfills. A landfill is a place where garbage is dumped in heaps from garbage trucks. Some sanitary landfills are lined on the bottom with a layer of clay soil covered with plastic.

Bulldozers push the garbage into neat piles. Then they cover it up with dirt so that it won't smell and so that animals and bugs will stay away.

Most people don't want landfills near where they live. And besides, there is so much garbage now that, in many places, there isn't enough room to bury all of it. Where can it all go?

One solution is to cut down on the amount of trash we make. We can do this by recycling some of our garbage to make it into new things. *Recycling* means reusing materials instead of throwing them away.

It takes a lot of trees and energy to make paper. In fact, people in the United States cut down 850 million trees to make paper products each year! When the trees are cut down, they are turned into wood chips. The wood chips are mixed with chemicals and water to make pulp. The pulp is spread out on a moving screen to make a thin layer of fibers. When the layer of fibers dries, it becomes paper.

Newspapers, boxes, magazines, and many other things are made from paper. When these things are through being used, they shouldn't be thrown away. RECYCLE!

Most towns and cities have recycling centers where bundles of old paper can be dropped off. In some places, trash collectors pick up the bundles of paper and take them away for recycling.

Old paper can be turned back into pulp and made into new recycled paper, using less energy than it takes to produce new paper from raw materials. Recycling paper saves trees and forests, which make oxygen and help keep the air clean. Saving forests protects the homes of many animals, too.

It takes lime, soda ash, and sand, called silica, to make glass. These three elements are mixed together and heated at a very high temperature to make a glassy liquid. Measured amounts, sometimes dyed, are dropped into forming machines, where the liquid hardens to make bottles and jars.

Many products come in glass bottles or jars. Sometimes, when they are through being used, they are just thrown away. It would take thousands of years for them to biodegrade at a landfill. Instead, these bottles and jars could be reused. RECYCLE!

Many bottles are returnable. A small deposit is paid when the bottles are bought. When they are returned, the deposit is paid back. Most of the time, the bottles are sent back to the company that made them, where they are sterilized and refilled. Sometimes the bottles are recycled into new glass.

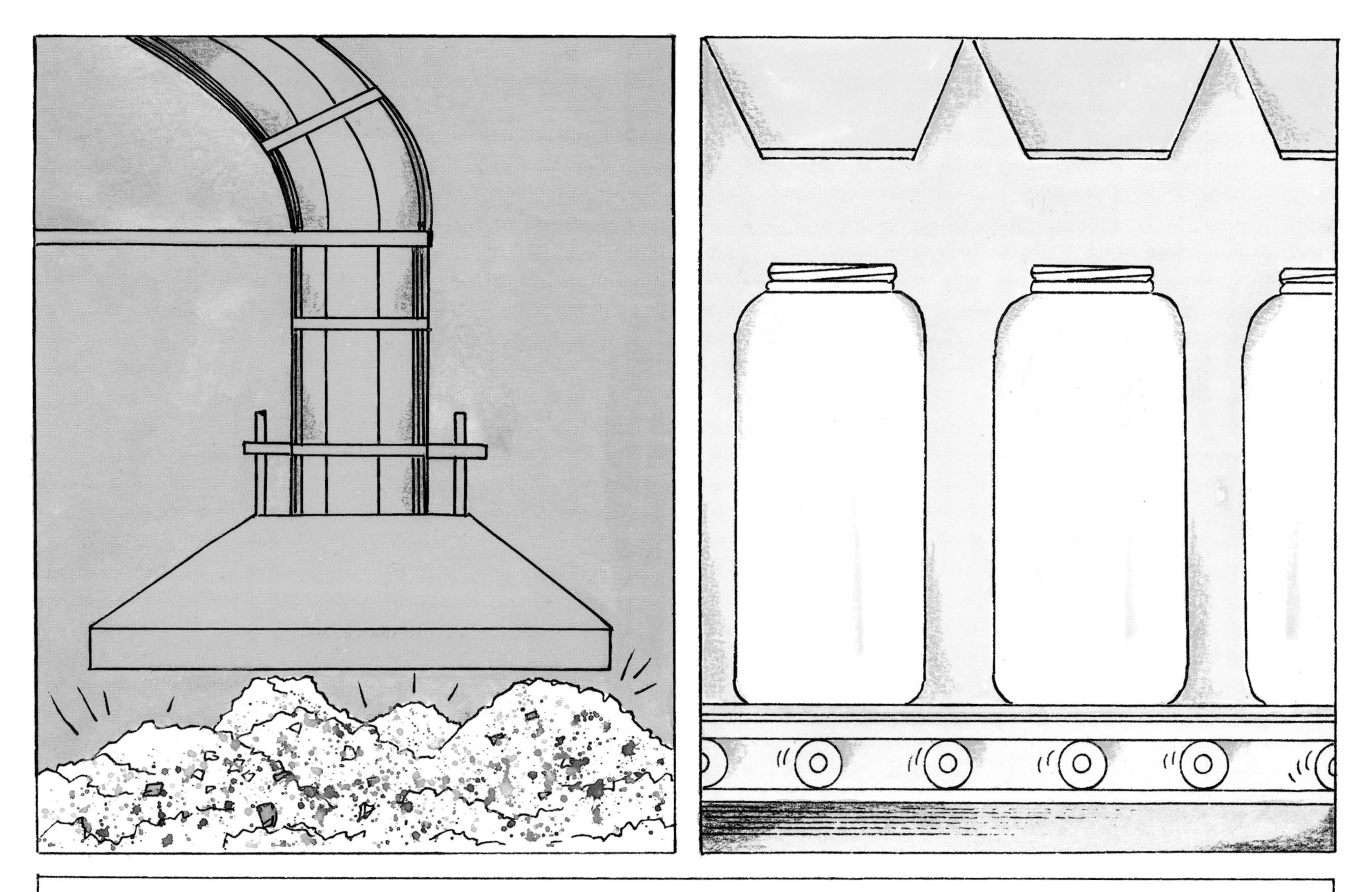

It takes much less energy and creates less pollution to make new glass from old glass. The glass is crushed and remelted. Next, recycled liquid glass is poured into forming machines and stamped into new glass products. The sand, lime, and soda ash don't have to be dug again, which would waste precious natural resources and destroy forests and fields.

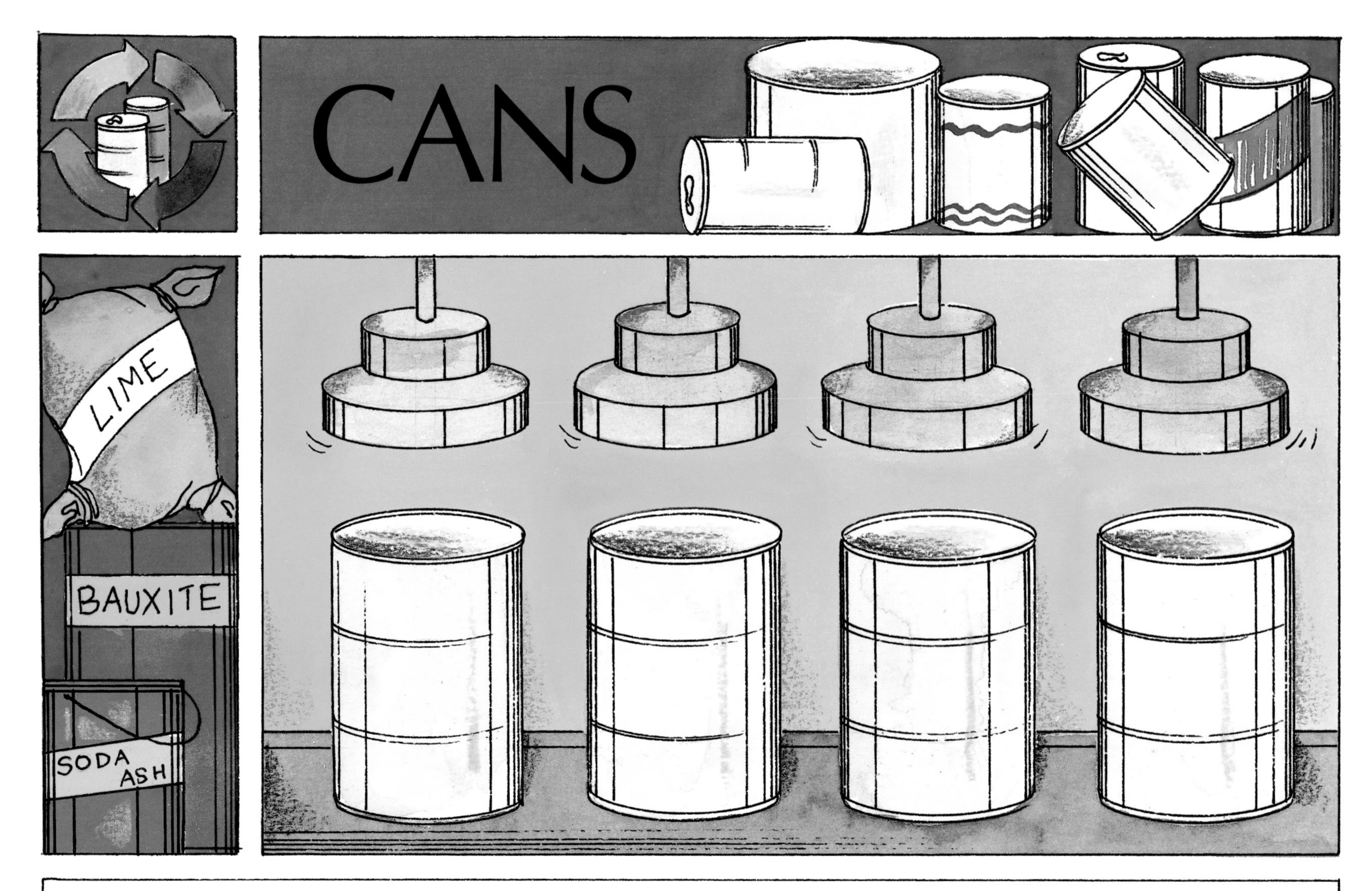

Most cans are made from aluminum. It takes many energy resources and creates pollution to produce pure aluminum. First, a mineral called bauxite (BOK-SITE) is mixed with soda ash and lime. When the mixture is put under pressure, aluminum is left as a by-product. Then the aluminum is heated and poured into molds to make cans.

Many products, such as soda and foods, are sold in aluminum cans. Often, when the cans are empty, they are just tossed away. It takes about 500 years for an aluminum can to biodegrade at a landfill. But these aluminum cans can be reused. RECYCLE!

Like glass bottles, many cans are returnable for a deposit refund. After the cans are returned, they are sent to plants to be ground into small metal chips. These chips are melted down and made into aluminum bars, which are pressed into thin sheets of recycled aluminum.

The sheets are then sold to can makers to be made into new cans.

It takes much less energy and makes much less pollution to make new aluminum from old aluminum. Natural resources such as bauxite, lime, and soda ash aren't taken from the earth to be used. Fields and forests are left alone.

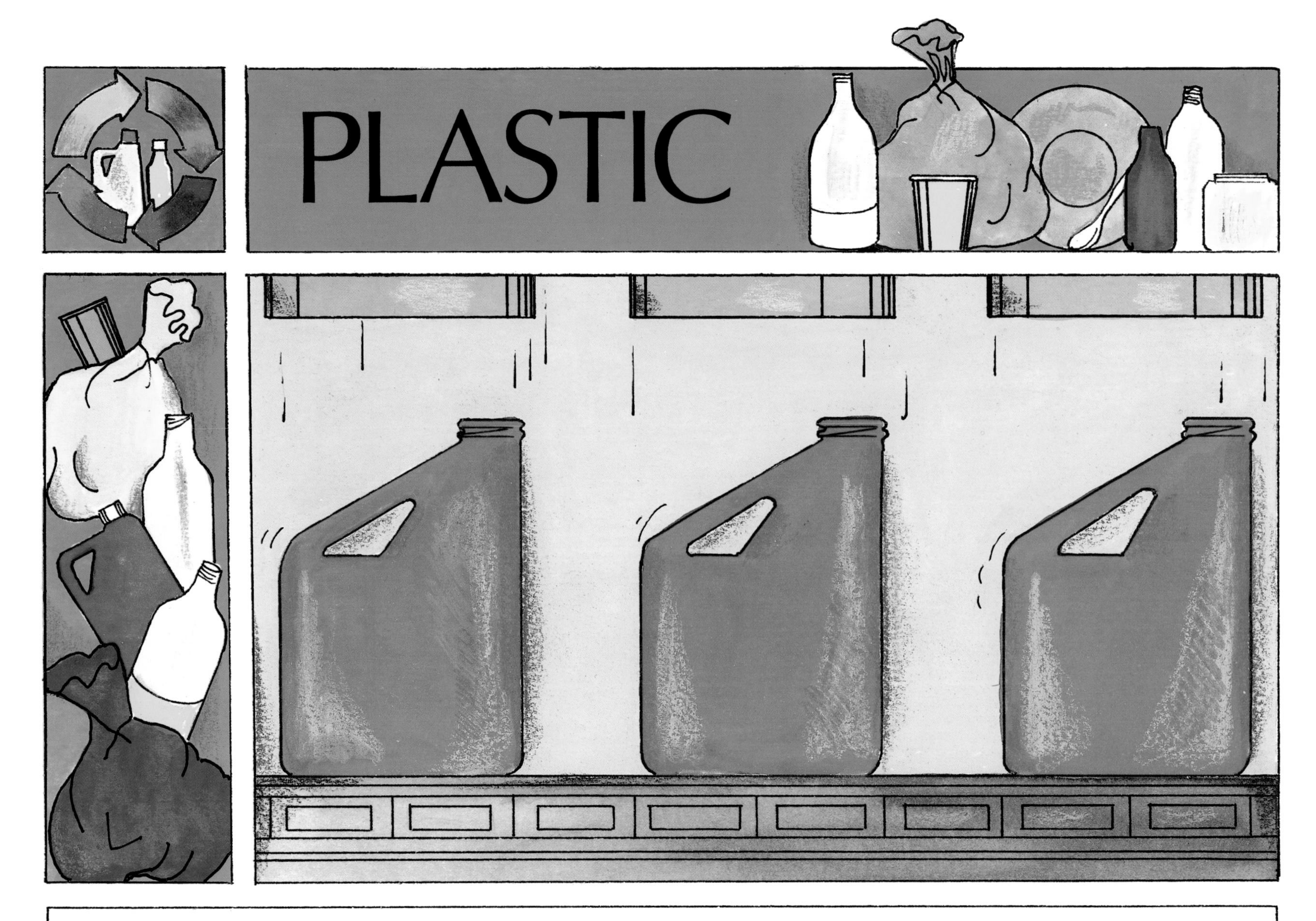

Plastic bottles. Plastic bags. Plastic plates. Plastic containers. Most plastic is made from molecules called polymers, which are derived from petroleum. The plastic is heated, sometimes dyed, and poured into molds.

A big problem with plastic is that it doesn't biodegrade. It can last forever! Instead of being allowed to fill landfills, litter roadsides, and harm wildlife, plastic can be recycled and used again. RECYCLE!

Like glass bottles and aluminum cans, some plastic bottles can be returned for a deposit refund. These bottles will be sent away to be recycled into new plastic products.

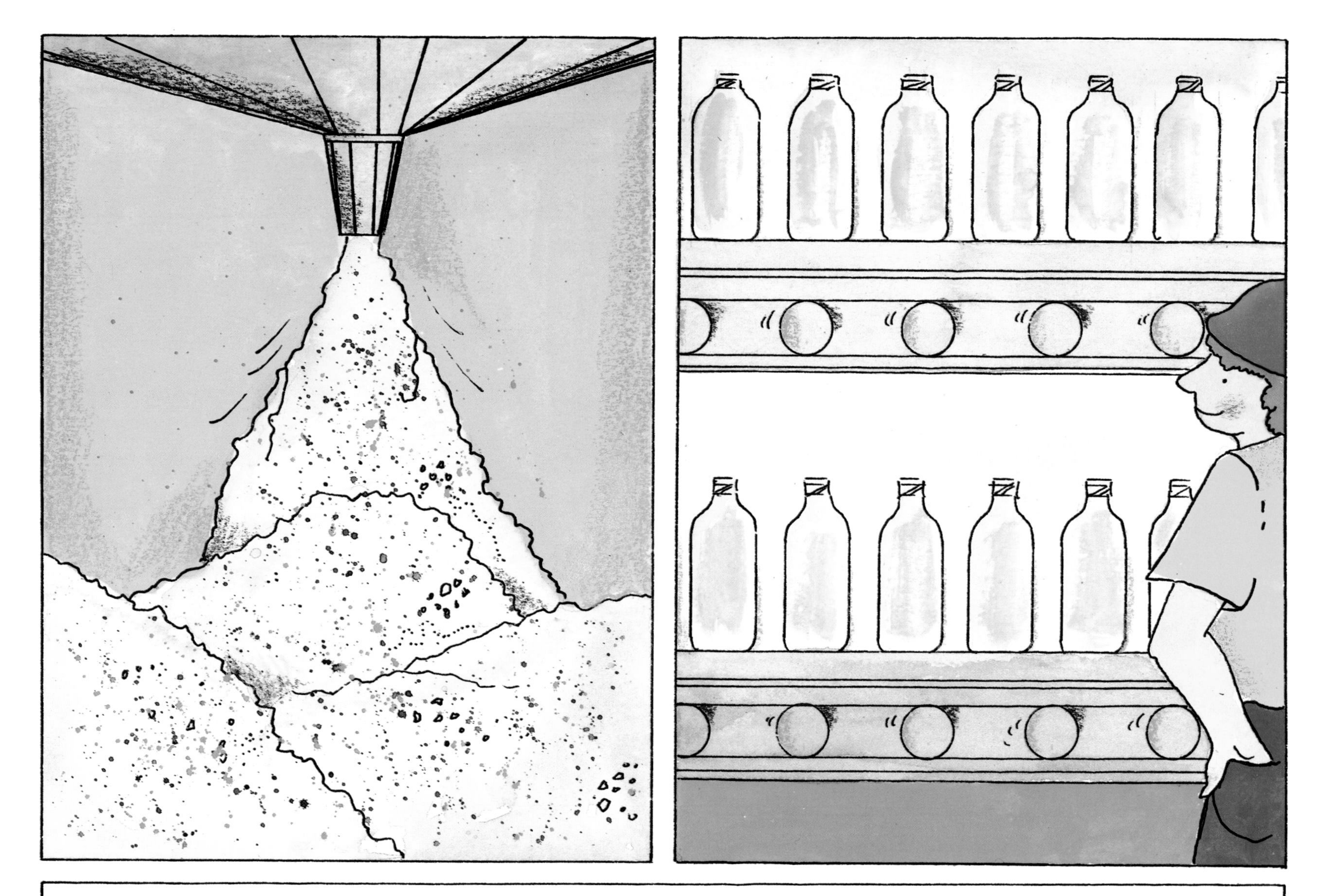

First the old plastic is cleaned. Then it is chopped up, melted down, and molded into new recycled products. Recycling plastic saves natural resources such as oil and prevents pollution caused by the manufacturing of plastic.

POLYSTYRENE

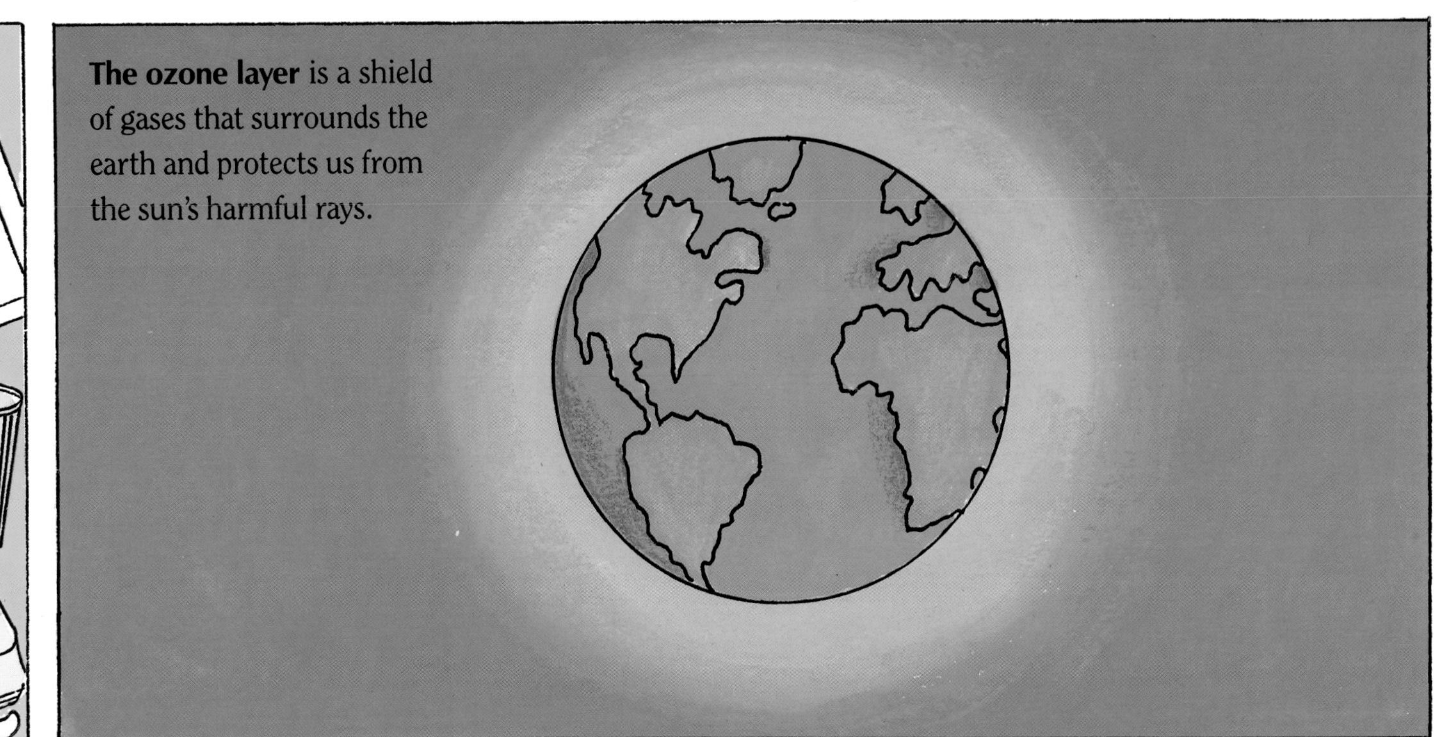

Many products are made from polystyrene (sometimes called Styrofoam™), such as cups, fast-food packaging, and packing materials. Some polystyrene is made using gases called chlorofluorocarbons (KLOR-O-FLOR-O-CAR-BUNS), also called CFCs. These chemicals are harmful to people and animals. When they are burned, they create poisonous gases and also harm the ozone layer surrounding our planet.

Unfortunately, it's cheaper to make new polystyrene than to recycle it. And there are few useful products that can be made from recycled polystyrene.

Plus, polystyrene is not biodegradable. Like plastic, it can last forever! The more polystyrene that is used and thrown away, the more garbage will sit in landfills for years and years.

Polystyrene is dangerous to sea animals, too. It floats on the water and sometimes looks like food. When sea animals try to eat it, their systems get clogged and often they starve to death.

If more and more people learn to recycle, there will be less garbage and our planet will be a safer and healthier place to live. Recycling can become a habit that is fun and easy. RECYCLE!

CAN YOU BELIEVE?...

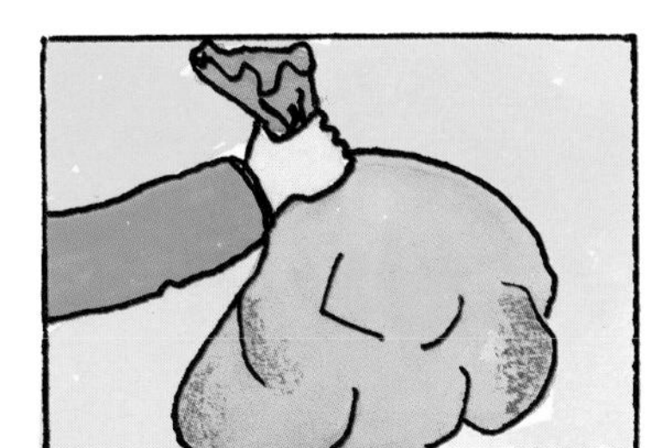

Each person in the United States throws out about four pounds of garbage every day.

New York City alone throws out enough garbage each day to fill the Empire State Building.

In one day, Americans get rid of 20,000 cars and 4,000 trucks and buses.

Fourteen billion pounds of trash is dumped into the ocean every year.

Forty-three thousand tons of food is thrown out in the United States each day.

Each hour, people in the United States use two and a half million plastic bottles.

People in the United States throw out about 270 million tires every year.

All the people in the United States make enough garbage each day to fill 100,000 garbage trucks.

In only one day, people in the United States toss out 15,000 tons of packaging material.

It takes 90 percent less energy to recycle an aluminum can than to make a new one.

Sixty-five billion aluminum soda cans are used each year.

The energy saved by recycling a glass bottle instead of making a new one would light a light bulb for four hours.

Every ton of paper that is recycled saves seventeen trees.

Only about one-tenth of all solid garbage in the United States gets recycled.

WHAT YOU CAN DO . . .

Begin your own home recycling center.

Organize a group outing to a park or beach to clean up litter.

Instead of using paper towels, use cloth towels, which can be washed and reused again and again.

Before you toss six-pack rings into the garbage, cut all the circles with a scissors so animals and birds can't get caught in them.

Instead of throwing out some things that you don't want anymore, see if someone else could use them. Try having a yard sale.

Keep a rag bag. Put old torn clothes in it and have a supply of rags to help clean house or use for messy projects.

When you go shopping, bring a cloth bag or recycle old brown paper bags by taking them with you.

Bring old books you don't want to your library. Maybe the library could use them.

Save paper. Use both sides of every sheet. Use recycled paper. If more of us use recycled paper, there will be a bigger demand for it.

And don't forget . . . RECYCLE!